TEXAS
A PICTURE MEMORY

Text
Bill Harris

Publishing Assistant
Edward Doling

Captions
Fleur Robertson

Editorial
Gill Waugh
Fleur Robertson

Design
Teddy Hartshorn

Production
Ruth Arthur
Sally Connolly
David Proffit
Andrew Whitelaw

Photography
Colour Library Books Ltd
FPG International

Picture Editor
Annette Lerner

Director of Production
Gerald Hughes

Commissioning Editor
Andrew Preston

Director of Publishing
David Gibbon

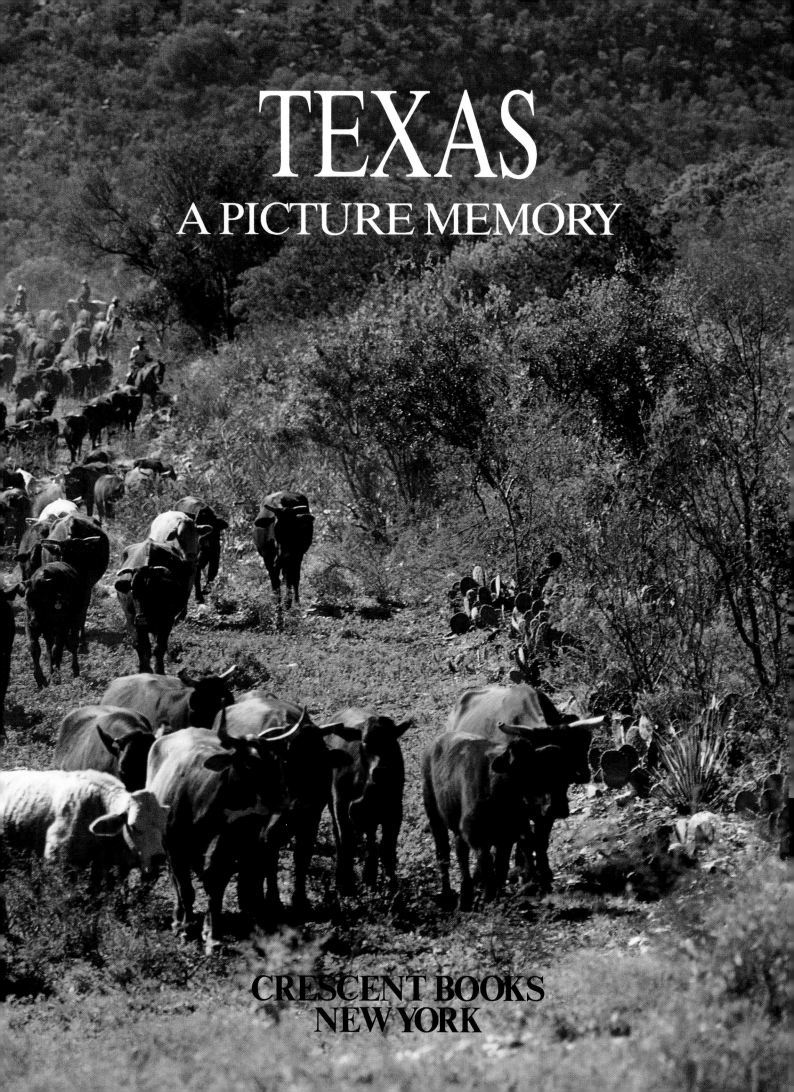

TEXAS
A PICTURE MEMORY

CRESCENT BOOKS
NEW YORK

Of all the images conjured by the name Texas, the Alamo is the most unforgettable. Without the memory, some say, Texas as we know it wouldn't exist. Texas children who never heard of the Battle of Agincourt and who suppose that D-Day must have had something to do with the founding of Dallas, can describe every detail of the short siege of a fortified mission at San Antonio more than 150 years ago.

Americans had been drifting into Spanish Texas for a dozen years before the confrontation at San Antonio, and bad blood between the fiercely independent men of the frontier and the Spanish, who considered themselves masters of all they surveyed, was inevitable. The Anglos had originally declared loyalty to Mexico as a condition of living there, but in 1832 they made it clear that they intended to live like Americans when they petitioned the Mexican Government to create a separate state for them and named Stephen F. Austin as their president. The recently elected Mexican president, General Antonio Lopez de Santa Anna, put down their claim as an illegal affront. But Austin went to Mexico City to plead their case. In twenty months of negotiation he was able to convince the authorities to allow more American immigration into Texas, but before he was able to leave for home, he was unceremoniously tossed into prison. By the time he was released eighteen months later, the enthusiasm for independence had caught fire in Texas and no one was in a more revolutionary frame of mind than Stephen F. Austin.

The shooting started not long after the harvesting was finished in 1835. A small Mexican force dispatched to confiscate a cannon at Gonzales was forced to retreat when the Texans opened fire. There was no turning back after that. The Anglos made their next move at Goliad and then, flushed with success, began marching on San Antonio. The army was little more than a mob. It had few trained officers and no experienced soldiers. Its artillery consisted of the lone cannon the Texans had defended at Gonzales, but that was left behind miles away mired in the mud. By the time they reached their destination, the ragtag force was mired in confusion too and when the military men among them refused a direct attack in favor of a long, dull siege, many of the volunteers decided to go home.

Meanwhile, word had crossed the Sabine River into United States territory that there was a war going on in Texas and hundreds of rough and ready characters decided to get in on the action. Soon there were more immigrants in the army than Texans, but if they weren't there to save their farms and families, they were more than willing to die for what seems to have been just the hell of it. Once the attack got under way, it took five days of house-to-house fighting to capture the Mexican stronghold behind the walls of the Alamo and a few days later they had driven all the Mexican troops out of Texas. It was a signal to the remaining Texans to go home, at least for the winter, and even their commander followed them.

The Anglo force had captured the two strongpoints necessary for the defense of Eastern Texas, and the Mexican Army was hundreds of miles away across hostile countryside. The Texans couldn't agree on how to govern themselves, but for a variety of reasons, nearly all of them personal to members of provisional government, they decided to take the war south of the Rio Grande into Mexico itself. Fortunately, there were some cool heads among them, including Governor Henry Smith, who had recently been impeached by the Council but held on to his office at the point of a gun. He thought a march into Mexico was foolishness and dispatched General Sam Houston to Goliad to attempt to stop the army in its tracks. Houston did better than that. He reinforced the garrison there, and sent Colonel James Bowie on to San Antonio to strengthen the fortress at the Alamo. But the army was itching for a fight. Out of 450 men ready to move south, only twenty-five were Texans and it was politely pointed out to Houston that he had no authority to command "American" volunteers. Houston responded by heading north to fight Indians.

When Jim Bowie arrived at the Alamo, he found the garrison reduced to 104 men with not a single Texan among them. Governor Smith responded by appointing Lieutenant Colonel Buck Travis to take charge at San Antonio and to take fifty Texas volunteers with him. Not long after he arrived, Davy Crockett, a frontier legend himself, came forward with a dozen of his pals from Tennessee. Bowie estimated that would take at least a thousand men to secure the mission-turned-fortress. The force would never be any larger than 150.

Meanwhile, General Santa Anna himself was leading a battle-hardened army of about 4,000 men toward San Antonio. The attack began before sunrise on March 6, 1836. Five hours later, at nine o'clock in the morning, it was all over. The Mexicans fought with tactics that had served Napoleon well in Europe, but the traditional artillery barrage failed because the big guns were stuck in the mud out of range, which meant that the general was forced to send his men in with fixed bayonets and scaling ladders. The defenders were armed with Kentucky long rifles, which most of them had learned to fire with deadly accuracy before they were as tall as the rifles were long. These hunting rifles also had a range three times that of the Mexican muskets and could be reloaded twice as fast. Mexican survivors later said that they were convinced there must have been at least a thousand men behind those walls. When they finally got inside and discovered they were mistaken, they came away with terrifying stories of these fierce giants they would forever after call Devil Texans. None of the devils survived, but the Mexican Army lost 1,600 of its best men and left behind another 500 wounded. If anyone had a reason to remember the Alamo, it was General Santa Anna.

While the battle was going on, a convention was being held at Washington-on-the-Brazos and, after a fiery speech by Sam Houston accusing his fellow Texans of making the Alamo possible by bickering rather than framing a government, it began to write a constitution for the independent Republic it had finally agreed to proclaim. As one of the men it designated to guide them, Sam Houston was made Commander in Chief of the Army. He was a perfect choice. Best of all, he looked the part. He was about six-feet, six-inches tall and weighed 240 pounds, every ounce of it muscle. He had steel gray eyes that could penetrate souls and a sense of fair play that inspired confidence in the most individualistic frontiersman.

Houston had drifted into Texas about twenty years earlier from Tennessee, where had had served as both Governor and as a member of Congress. He had also been a major general in the state militia and a certified hero in the Creek Indian uprising. Before leaving for Texas, his life had been ruined when his wife left him after three months of marriage, and when he arrived there, he went to live among the Cherokee Indians, some of whom he had known back in Tennessee, but who now came to know him as "Big Drunk." His life changed again when the Texas Anglos began talking about independence and he became one of their most ardent supporters.

His initial forays against the Mexicans as Commander in Chief of the Texas Army were uninspiring. His men were untrained. But little by little, Houston taught them how to fight and when Santa Anna was properly lulled into complacency, Houston allowed himself to be "trapped" at the San Jacinto River. The Texans were outnumbered, but determined. They mounted a surprise attack and it was over in minutes. With shouts of "Remember the Alamo!" the Mexican force was overrun. Only two Texans died; Santa Anna buried 630 men and another 700 were taken prisoner. And for the people of the Republic of Texas, the best part was that nearly all the men who had seized the day were their fellow citizens. Most of the adventurers who had joined them a few months earlier had gone home again.

Sociologists attempting to explain the self-image Texans have developed over the years often trace it back to Sam Houston and the defenders of the Alamo. The high drama of securing the Republic and the experience of existing for ten years as an independent nation is a powerful legacy that sets Texas apart from other states. As the last true frontier on the American continent, its families still share a tradition of self-reliance and its corollary, self-importance, that seem almost quaint to other Americans. They are as all-American as the rest of us, but even relative newcomers from the Northeast don't mind telling you that first and foremost they are Texans.

Almost eighty percent of all Texans live in cities, but even people whose homes are in Houston high-rises have an uncommonly strong feeling for the land. It's as if they themselves had experienced the long struggle to secure it.

Land is what Texas is all about. Once Texas became the 29th state at the end of 1845, Americans began pouring across the Sabine River in record numbers. About ninety percent of them came from the Old South, with Tennessee and Alabama contributing nearly half of that percentage and Georgia and Mississippi close behind. When Stephen Austin came back from Mexico, he had gone east to recruit new settlers and when statehood became a reality, the new government followed his lead. Every newly created territory from Eden to Israel has owed its existence to populating the land with as many people as possible and Texas was no exception. Its treasury was virtually empty, but it had land in abundance and that became the lure. The state's constitution gave every Texan family 4,000 acres and stipulated that any immigrant family would be given 1,280 acres with no strings attached. This was much more land than any farm family could develop by itself, but they were free to resell it and there were plenty of speculators willing to buy it. Yet whether they sold all of it or part of it, every family in Texas had the opportunity to own a substantial piece of land, and that was a very powerful incentive for settlement.

Even though the lure was strong and immigration from Europe into the United States was at its peak in the 1840s, relatively few foreign-born people found their way into Texas. By 1860, there were only about 30,000 of them and, like the immigrants from the various states, they tended to live apart from the the general population in their own communities. In the mid nineteenth century, assimilation wasn't part of the Texas ethic. That would come later. In the meantime, where a man settled in Texas had a lot to do with where he came from. In some places the culture of the Old South prevailed, in others arrivals from Missouri and other border states added a Western flavor, and in the process the outlook of the people themselves made east and west Texas as different from each other as Virginia and Kentucky. The European-born and newcomers from the Northeast flocked together in the southwest where they became the new state's leading merchants and its

major political influence.

Most of the European immigrants became Anglicized quickly. But there was one important exception. In 1842, a group of German noblemen began dreaming of establishing a *Kleines Deutschland* in America. The Republic of Texas seemed to be the ideal place to make the dream come true. The climate was good, it had ports to receive German imports and just enough disorganization in its government to make it possible for better organized people to take charge. They recruited thousands of future Texans by promising them free passage and free land, even free houses. But they had bought land they had never seen. Worse, they had bought it from a couple of speculators who didn't have the right to sell it.

While the duped noblemen were trying to figure out how to make the best of a bad thing, hundreds of their countrymen died of fever and starvation in ramshackle camps near Galveston. Finally, led by Otfried Hans, Frieherr Von Meusebach, who fortuitously changed his name to John, they went on foot 300 miles from Indianola to the place they called New Braunfels. It wasn't a Garden of Eden, but with work they knew they could make it one.

Meusebach went to work negotiating with the Comanche Indians for more land, something most Texans considered an act very close to suicide. The Comanche were well known as the most savage Indian tribe in North America, even the dreaded Apaches avoided them. And though they didn't seem to like any other people, the ones they hated most were Texans and Mexicans. But fortunately for the Germans, the Comanche chiefs recognized them as a separate tribe and agreed to share their land with them. The truce lasted through the Indian depredations that made life difficult for most other Texans, so the most serious problem the Germans faced was taming the land itself.

In the years before the Civil War an average of 200 Texans were killed by Indians each year. Many more were tortured and lived to tell about it. When Mirabeau Buonaparte Lamar replaced Sam Houston as President of the Texas Republic he said "The White Man and the Red Man cannot dwell in harmony together, Nature forbids it." Nothing short of an all-out war to drive them off the land was required, he believed. It became the longest war in American history, lasting almost forty years and killing thousands on both sides.

But Texans had other things on their mind at the same time. From the very beginning, Texas has had an unusually high literacy rate. When it became a state, ninety-five percent of its citizens could read and write. It had more than seventy newspapers, which appealed to the passionate love of politics that seems to be a prerequisite for being a Texan. And virtually no town was without a school, usually one established and paid for by its own citizens. Their textbooks were frequently Bibles. Every family had one, so it helped cut down on expenses. The result was that almost any Texan could hold his own in an argument by quoting Scripture. And then, as now, there are few things a Texan enjoys more than a lively argument.

Almost any outlandish thing you hear about a typical Texan probably has some basis in truth. As a race, they're as ornery as a longhorn steer, as tough as an oil-field roughneck, as sweet as a field of bluebonnets. Though they may earn their living programming computers, they go to their offices in high-heeled boots and broad-brimmed hats. Though they might have a Ph.D. from the University of Texas, they still drink their beer from long-necked bottles and drive downtown in a pickup truck with a rack of rifles in the rear window. If they develop a passing interest in the latest dance craze from Brazil, they know in their hearts it will never compare to the Texas two-step. And if baseball is the national pastime, and Texas has two professional teams, almost no pastime stirs a Texan quite like football. But of all the things we all accept as articles of faith about Texans, the one that doesn't wash is that they are nearly all millionaires. The fact is, there are more millionaires in Minnesota than in Texas, where the average per capita income is $14,640. But as any Texan will tell you, you don't need much to find the good life in the Lone Star State. Like the mustang horses that made development possible, they thrive and prosper on very little.

The common denominator in the Texas personality is probably found in the name itself. In the early sixteenth century, when the Spaniards moved north of the Rio Grande in search of gold, they made contact with a tribe of Caddoan Indians in the Texas Panhandle. They were unusually friendly, especially compared to the Apaches the Conquistadores had already met. Impressed, the explorers described them with one of their own words, *Teychas,* which means "friends." In Spanish, the word took on a "j" sound and became *Tejas.* In written form, the "j" became an "x" and this friendly place in the Southwest became known as Texas.

The best part is that the word still fits. You can still walk into Billy Bob's in Fort Worth and feel like a native. You can go to the Scholz Bier Garten in Austin, which still claims, as it did in the 1860s, to be "The oasis of Texas' most exciting intellectuals … and their woman," and join in the singing even if you're tone deaf. You can exchange Aggie jokes or you can thrill at the recent accomplishments of the Texas A&M football team. Or you can take part in a philosophical discussion that might be like the one that took place back in the Seventies between Fletcher Boone and Martin Wigginton over the nature of man. Man is just interested in bread alone, stated Wigginton. But he needs beauty, too, argued Boone. The debate raged through fifteen rounds of beer before it ended in a draw. None of the spectators had their opinions changed, but they all agreed it was one of the best debates they had ever seen. It was high praise in a place where debating is high art.

But in the end, it didn't matter. If man is just interested in bread alone, there is opportunity aplenty in Texas. But if he also needs beauty to make him happy, there is an also an abundance of that in the Lone Star State.

Facing page: flagpoles outside Dallas City Hall that reach a height of eighty feet.

Below left: Municipal Plaza Park, Dallas. Above, above left and facing page top: Reunion Tower, a famous Dallas landmark, and (below) the spiral Chapel of Thanksgiving, which contains French stained glass, in Dallas' Thanks-Giving Square, a quiet retreat in the center of the city. Facing page bottom: the Doubletree Hotel gleams in the twilight of a summer's night in Dallas, its spherical form reflecting its neighbors.

Below: the Texas State Fair in the Dallas park (bottom right) of the same name built in 1936 for the Texas Centennial Exposition. The park houses permanent exhibitions, such as the Dallas Aquarium, Science Place and the Texas Hall of State. The fair, the nation's largest annual state exposition, is held in October. Below right: the Texas Stadium, home of the Dallas Cowboys, at Irving, near west Dallas. Right: the Galleria, one of four major shopping malls in Dallas (overleaf). It is always possible to shop in the city, even on Sundays.

Dallas' Swiss Avenue Historic District was established in 1973 and was the first of its kind in the metropolis. The area contains approximately 200 beautifully preserved homes built by early leading citizens of the city. Below left: the dignified interior and (facing page bottom) the imposing façade of Aldredge House and (above left, above, left and below) the light and gracious decor of Collins House, both on Swiss Avenue. A combination of architectural styles exists here, the Italianate (facing page top) being the most common.

Below and bottom right: distinctive brickwork on Main Street, Fort Worth (below right), thirty miles from Dallas. Such is the size of each city that they are nearly one metropolis now. Lying midway between them is Arlington's Six Flags Over Texas theme park (right) which lists among its attractions breathtaking rides, such as on the Shock Wave double loop roller coaster, and a 200-foot parachute drop.

Facing page top: elegant Howard-Dickinson House, Henderson, and (facing page bottom and above) the distinctive House of Seasons in Jefferson, both in East Texas. Right: the East Texas Oil Museum, Kilgore, where the town's oil-boom days are recreated. Above right: Old Fort Parker State Historic Site at Groesbeck, site of a Comanche raid in 1836. Below: the Old County Courthouse in Marshall and (below right) a restored nineteenth-century cabin at Nacogdoches. Overleaf: cypress swamps in Caddo Lake State Park northeast of Marshall.

This page and overleaf: Houston's business district. Houston was named for Sam Houston, who led Texans to independence at the Battle of San Jacinto in 1836. Today San Jacinto Battleground Park (facing page top) surrounds a 570-foot-high monument commemorating this famous battle against the Mexicans. The view from the top of the column is superb. A museum depicting the region's history is housed in the base of the monument. U.S.S. Texas (facing page bottom), veteran of two world wars, is moored near the battleground.

Facing page top: the black column of Houston's Allied Bank Building seen from Sam Houston Historical Park and (facing page bottom and overleaf) the distinctive shapes of the city's jewelled skyscrapers at night. Houston grew initally as an important exporter of cotton, but once oil was discovered in Texas, refining soon became a major industry here. Below: the spacious atrium of the city's luxurious Hyatt Regency Hotel.

Ashton Villa (these pages) in Galveston was built as one of the first Italianate mansions in Texas by James Moreau Brown. Brown was a mason who designed and built the house himself in 1859, even going to the length of making the bricks on site. It is said that the surrender of Galveston was accepted here in 1865, and during yellow fever epidemics in the town after the War between the States the house also served as a hospital.

Below: an oil tanker approaches Corpus Christi, a major deepwater port and one of the ten busiest in the country. The city is beautifully situated on the Gulf of Mexico and renowned for its deep-sea fishing and superb yachting. Bottom right and overleaf: Corpus Christi marina. Right: Halfmoon Reef Lighthouse near Port Lavaca and (below right) leisure attractions at Port Aransas, both seaside resorts on the Gulf.

Below: four-story Fulton Mansion in Fulton, built by George Fulton in 1876 and a showpiece of its time, and (facing page bottom) the Simon Guggenheim House, one of many old houses in the Corpus Christi Heritage Park. The Simon Guggenheim was built in 1905 by a man who arrived in the town with $40 and struck it rich in the petroleum industry. Facing page top: Yellow House in Rockport.

These pages: San Antonio, the only major city in the state that existed before Texas won its independence from Mexico. Facing page top: the Melodrama Theater in Hemisfair Park and (facing page bottom) the Arneson Theater, part of San Antonio's famous River Walk. This open-air theater has its small and simple stage on one side of the San Antonio River and its seating on the other. Below: the Spanish Colonial architecture of the Mission San José y San Miguel de Aguayo. This mission, built between 1768 and 1782, is one of the oldest and finest churches in Texas and the most elaborate of the eighteenth-century missions preserved in the city in the San Antonio Missions National Historical Park. Right: the Alamo Cenotaph, designed by Pompeii Coppini, which honors the heroic defenders of the Alamo. Probably all of the 188 rebel sharpshooters could have escaped through the Mexican lines, since the siege was not a tight one, but instead they chose to stay and fight, facing certain death for the sake of Texas' independence. In the end, the Americans killed 600 Mexicans before the Alamo was taken and they were slaughtered. Their sacrifice bought time for Sam Houston's larger army, and at San Jacinto, several weeks later, the Mexicans would hear the vengeful cry, "Remember the Alamo!" Overleaf: the Alamo Chapel, built on the battlesite at San Antonio.

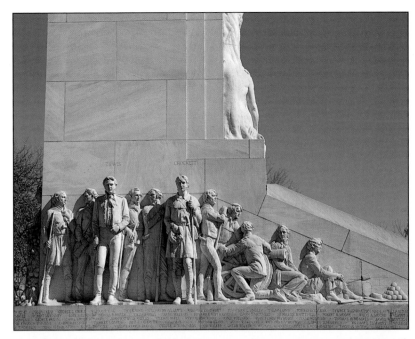

41

Between 1938 and 1941 the Works Progress Administration completed an ambitious landscaping of the banks of the San Antonio River as part of a flood control project in San Antonio. The beautiful River Walk (below, below right and bottom right) was designed by Robert H. H. Hugman to create a "quaint atmosphere" reminiscent of classic Spanish cities. Right: San Antonio at night seen from the Tower of the Americas.

Below: an equestrian bronze of a Texas Ranger guards the ·steps to the Texas State Capitol in Austin, while the Goddess of Liberty stands atop the dome. Facing page: (top) the imposing First Methodist Church on Lavaca Street and (bottom) the Senate Chamber of the State Capitol, both in Austin.

Below: the Lyndon Baines Johnson Presidential Library and Museum, Austin, which traces the career of President Johnson from his time in the House of Representatives through his Presidency, assumed after President Kennedy's assassination. Right: Austen's Congress Avenue Bridge spanning Texas' Colorado River, (below right) University of Texas Tower and the Lichfield Memorial Fountain in Austin (bottom right).

49

These pages: a variety of restored Texan homes, both grand and lowly. Above: the Neill-Cochran House, built in Austin in 1852 and designed by Abner Cook. The National Trust for Historic Preservation called this mansion "a jewel and perfect example of the Texas version of the Greek Architectural Revival in the South." Today it is a museum furnished with antiques spanning three centuries. Above left: the Governor's Mansion in Austin. Governor Pease, who was responsible for commissioning the house in 1856, was criticized for his extravagance. Such a fine edifice for a head of state was considered inappropriate at the time. Today, however, the mansion is held to be one of the loveliest in Austin and, not surprisingly, most governors since Pease have been happy to live there. Left: the Swisher-Scott House, also known as Sweetbrush, and (below and overleaf) the magnificent Shriver House, both Austin mansions of distinction. Below left: President Johnson's ranch, known during Johnson's Presidency as the "Texas White House," and (facing page top) a reconstruction of the President's birthplace beside the Pedernales River, both near the Lyndon B. Johnson State Historical Park in the Texas Hill Country. Facing page bottom: L.B.J.'s restored boyhood home in Johnson City, parts of which are also administered by the state park. The President's family had lived in the Hill Country of Texas for more than a century, and even while he held the highest office in the land Johnson would take time to return to these hills, the place he always considered to be home. In accordance with his wishes, he was buried here in a simple grave in the Johnson family cemetery.

Below: sunset over Inks Lake, one of a series of lakes lying south of the Buchanan Dam near Kingsland. Right: granite in Enchanted Rock State Park near Fredericksburg and (below right) Monahans Sandhills State Park near Monahans. Bottom right: the Praire Dog Town Fork of the Red River carving the Palo Duro Canyon (overleaf) in Palo Duro Canyon State Park.

Facing page: (top) downtown El Paso and (below) the city's Civic Center. Above and right: the Amarillo Livestock Auctions, which are held at the Western Stockyards in Amarillo (below right) every week. Above right: the National Ranching Heritage Center, part of the Texas Tech University, Lubbock. This complex is the most comprehensive record of ranch architecture in the state, over thirty structures having been moved to the center from all over Texas. Below: Fredericksburg, a town in Central Texas.

Above left: a parched West Texas landscape near Hot Springs and (left) clouds parting to reveal Pulliam Ridge above the Rio Grande, which forms the border between Mexico and the United States and later meets Lake Amistad (last page). Above: rugged peaks near Panther Pass, (below) Santa Elena Canyon, (facing page top) silhouettes of the Chisos Mountains and (facing page bottom) the Window seen from the Basin, all in Big Bend National Park in West Texas. Overleaf: El Capitan Peak in Guadalupe Mountains National Park (below left).